L♥VE
QUOTES
for me

L♥VE QUOTES
for me

BRENT
ARMBRISTER

Charleston, SC
www.PalmettoPublishing.com

Love Quotes For Me

Copyright © 2022 by Brent Armbrister

All rights reserved

First Edition

Paperback ISBN: 979-8-8229-0714-0
eBook ISBN: 979-8-8229-0715-7

Dedication

This book is dedicated to you who want to feel the power of love. This book is love in word form for you to experience the love sensation.

Give me you.

Just when I thought I had
all that I needed,
here you come, completing me.

I guess this means that.....we're in love.

I will never stop loving you.

Talking to you uplifts my spirit.

I kiss my phone every time
I see your picture.

The smallest interaction with you
brings me the biggest joy.

Hope you had a good night's sleep and
I hope you have an amazing day.

Let me be the pillow
where your love rests its head.

I just want you to have a great day.

You have the face of an angel.

What's your favorite food?
What kind of stuff do you like to do?
I want to know all about you.

My heart is yours.

It's just something about you.......

Brent Armbrister

Today I was daydreaming
about your smiling face.

I like you.

You're so pretty.

Our love is destined to be.

I don't know what you want me to do
but I can't stop loving you.

Your concern for me is what lets me
know that our love is real.

There are so many reasons to love you
that I can pick a different one every day.

A lifetime of love is our gift from God.

I want to do things for you.

Your love caresses my soul.

I can't help it if I'm full of love.
I just want to give some to you.

Do you love me?

Your vibe is my drug.

Take in this moment we share.

Together we can take on the world.

Your touch is my medicine.

You saved me from myself.

You're the most beautiful person
that I've ever seen.

I want to vibe with you.

I'm going crazy over you.

You're so pretty they should
name a flower after you.

You made me who I am today.

Me, kissing on your neck.

I appreciate you.

You have to open up and
allow me to love you.

You have that vibe that
I want to experience.

When I'm with you I feel free.

Sending you kisses.

I know you are, wherever you are,
looking sexy.

I want to connect with you.

Hope you had a good day.

You deserve my love.

When I'm close to you time stops.

Why do I wake up with you on my mind?

I'm blessed to have you in my life.

Do you know what I noticed about you?
I noticed that you love for real.
You take this love thing seriously.
That's why I want your love.

9 798822 907140